# PLOT AND
# COUNTER-PLOT

for Alan
fellow-plotter
and
HeppenStancer
with love
Dell
x

By the same author

*Mr and Mrs Philpott on Holiday at Auchterawe & Other Poems*, Kettillonia, 2002

*Starlight on Water,* Rialto Press, 2003

*Unsuitable Poems,* HappenStance, 2005

*The Unread Squirrel*, HappenStance, 2009

# PLOT AND COUNTER-PLOT

Helena Nelson

*Helena Nelson*

Shoestring Press

Printed by imprintdigital
Upton Pyne, Exeter
www.imprintdigital.net

Typeset by Nathanael Burgess
info@shoestring-press.com

Published by Shoestring Press
19 Devonshire Avenue, Beeston, Nottingham, NG9 1BS
(0115) 925 1827
www.shoestringpress.co.uk

First published 2010
© Copyright: Helena Nelson
The moral right of the author has been asserted.
ISBN 978-1-907356-19-3

# ACKNOWLEDGEMENTS

Thanks are due to editors of the following publications in which some of these poems first appeared: *Ambit, Assent* (also its predecessor, *Poetry Nottingham*), *Hawai'i Review 64, P N Review, Smiths Knoll, Snakeskin* (ezine), *The Dark Horse, The London Magazine, The North, The Rialto.*

# Contents

The Need ................................................ 1
With My Mother, Missing the Train ..... 2
Your Nose ............................................ 3
The Beautiful Day ................................ 4
Imagery ................................................ 5
Old Wife's Tale ..................................... 6
Messenger ............................................ 7
Straws .................................................. 8
Inside Her House He Built His House of Tears ..... 9
Helen Davies ....................................... 10
Work .................................................... 11
Accommodation ................................. 12
Impasse ............................................... 13
After .................................................... 14
Rehearsal ............................................ 15
State of Grace ..................................... 16
The Answer .......................................... 18
Teller ................................................... 19
The Visitors ......................................... 20
Pattern ................................................ 22
Comforters .......................................... 23
Putting Words in Your Mouth ............. 24
The Ballad of Ballantoul Burn ............ 26
The Good Wife ..................................... 27
Gone .................................................... 28
Garden of Love .................................... 30
The Kiss ............................................... 31
Remembering the Way ......................... 32
Gate Keeper ........................................ 33
Felis Infelix ......................................... 34
Plainsong ............................................ 35

The Size of Grief     36
Proof     37
Auchterawe Wood     38
Just This     39
At Last     40
A Picture of Forgetting     41
Landlubber's Song     42
The Hill     44
Seer     46
Blight     47
Duel     48
Fairy Tale     49
Preoccupation     50
Secret     51
Epistle to Angus Calder     52
The Book of the Night     53
Making the Bed     54

If my mind can't see
where my brain can't go

I won't see I don't see,
won't know I don't know.

# The Need

a need
of nobody at all
grew slow
and first quite small
and tried to find a person
who could echo such an ache

but as it grew
nobody it knew
could answer such and echo such
an incompleteness

and so the need
found in itself
a kind of sweetness

# With My Mother, Missing the Train

She was always late. At the final minute
we'd run for the city train, which roared right past,
its line of faces scanning us not in it.
The world was turned to terror by the blast
of hot departing wheels. Air seized my mother,
crushing her flustered skirts into a flurry
with me there clinging. *Hush, there'll be another,*
she'd say to keep me calm. *No need to worry.*
But there was a need. The speed of things was true
and rushing traffic urged us both ahead.
I wanted to race again, to burst right through
and make the great train wait. She never said
that missing things was serious, till I grew.
She held my hand more tightly than I knew.

## Your Nose

The blowing of your nose was a trumpet
thrilling the house, rocking from cellar to attic,
shaking the stairs and banisters. It was a strict
aquiline beak that you called 'Roman' – at least
it would have been if you hadn't broken it
and crooked it sideways in the mending. You ate
*Club* biscuits in majestic bites, then hooked
the wrapper over your royal snout and snorted
until we giggled. Quick to condemn, you sniffed
with curling lip at fads and fatuous fools.
Even in later years your grand-dad trunk
inhaled the world as fiercely, quivering over
a cut glass filled with amber. Presence flared
from your nostrils; little children warmed themselves
by dragon flames that lasted and lasted. Yes.

# The Beautiful Day

On the beautiful, beautiful day
nobody moped or cried
or said that the lemonade
was too expensive to buy

and the sun was not too hot
and the wind was not too strong
and the sandwiches tasted right
and the journey was not too long

and the river was bright and cold
and we paddled and splashed in fun
and were good – as good as gold –
and we shared the gold we spun

and when it was time for home
nobody seemed to mind
and the car was snug and warm
and we all sang 'Clementine'

and our darling beds were fine
with sheets fresh-ironed like new
and we slept from dusk to dawn –
it was beautiful, and it was true.

# Imagery

Love is like riding a bicycle of light
spinning on two great wheels of moon and sun,
clean rain in your hair, and the air
kissing your face and tugging your clothes,
balance as sharp as a rush of stars.

You would ride forever
but it is only a simile.
Love is not a bicycle. Love
waits in a country lane.
Love will unseat you.

## Old Wife's Tale

There was an old woman who lived in a shoe.
What could she do? What could she do?
She filled it with children from top to toe.
All this you know, all this you know.
You know the old woman, and she knows you.

There was an old woman lived in the snow.
What did she know? What did she know?
She made up a snowman. He looked as though
He was warm and white as truth, and so
Where did he go? Where did he go?

There was an old story, and this is true:
A woman who loved and she loved you.
She shouldn't have spoken, but speak she did
And the shoe was stitched to the other foot
So she had to go. What could she do?

Nothing under the sun is new –
Another old woman, another old shoe,
Another decision to mend and make do
With a song to carry the story through
To you, my darling. To you, to you.

# Messenger

The man gets out of a white taxi.
His hair is on fire.
With his hands he says –
*Can anyone hear?*

The police arrive and fire fighters.
The man's hair lights up the square.
He's radiant with joy.
His gestures tell stories.

The police won't listen.
They aren't happy.
One of them bawls,
'Turn on the hoses!'

*Something* – he signs
– *something amazing*
silenced by water,
volumes of water.

## Straws

*What is thy beloved more than another beloved, O thou fairest among women?* Song of Solomon 5:9

You want to love but it's too difficult.
The one you want has two relationships
and both his ships will sink. He lets you down
again. You disembark and start to drink.
The drink will sink you too. Its cordial warmth
releases words – you hate him and you love
your loveless life without him and you hate
the lies of sailors and don't you just long
for the day he'll land at your side and beg
for love? 'Oh listen please – I really meant – '
he'll say. 'Go fuck yourself!' you scream
and smash the door into his hateful face
but you are drunk and love him still, and still
you want to love but it's too difficult.

## Inside Her House He Built His House of Tears

According to his law, every door
stays shut. Inside, the chill is dangerous:
it freezes the balls off those visitors
who still call. They don't stay long. Icicles
drip on their heads and there's nowhere
dry to sit down. In the absence of chairs
he offers them one of his bicycles
as he free-wheels past. His mother despairs.
So what? He drinks. Don't expect him to care –
bring an umbrella. He made excuses
once. Now he savours bad form, refuses
all invitations. He intends to tear
the phone out, swing from the chandeliers.

# Helen Davies[*]

What became of the poet's wife
after the poet died
is hard to tell. She moved away.
She may (or may not) have cried.

Nobody wrote her biography.
She didn't talk to the press.
Was there a friend before the end?
All we can do is guess.

She wasn't partial to reading.
Davies stayed on the shelf.
How glad she was Young Emma
hadn't exposed herself.

Outliving him by forty years
she went her private way.
Did poetry ever comfort her?
Probably not, I'd say.

*Young Emma,* a novel by the poet W H Davies, was withdrawn from
publication at the request of his wife, Helen. Both believed the true
account of their meeting and subsequent marriage had been destroyed.
Younger than Davies by nearly 30 years, Helen was working the streets as a
'courtesan' when Davies picked her up at a bus stop. The marriage lasted
until the poet's death seventeen years later; Helen Davies did not re-marry.
Cape published *Young Emma* in 1980 after her death.

## Work

Born in the dark
shimmering, pure,
it wakes you at dawn.
Everything else is dirty beside it –
the swings, the play-park, the shoddy gardens.

Cold in its beauty, its calculation,
work shines clean.
Driven honour, harder than love.
Begin, begin.

# Accommodation

Yes, that part of me is reserved.
It is a sleeping chrysalis
between the neatly folded towels
in the airing cupboard, alone
in the warm dark. It has gone
to where a woman keeps her work.

No. Neither for your open vowels
nor brown eyes that have observed
much, will I tender this.

## Impasse

If you would say, *I'm sorry,*
I would say, *It's all right,*
but you won't – or can't.

Eventually it's night.
We try, and fail, to sleep.
Only the rain speaks

and its tale is ours to keep:
it tells of isolation
and the separateness of souls.

No kind of consolation,
no lamp, no guiding star.
You must be very afraid.

We are as we are.
I will unmake what's made.

# After

She doesn't yearn for him
as he yearns for her

but in the night
when the stars grow dim

and he turns to her,
she turns to him.

# Rehearsal

You wake one morning feeling not right.
You wonder what it means.
It may be something, may be nothing.

You make a cup of tea and look at the sky.
The feeling recedes.
The sky is blank with smudges of grey.

You drink the tea. What will it be like
waking one day and feeling wrong,
having the feeling not go away –

having it mean everything?
You finish your tea.
You wash the cup with care.

# State of Grace

Something was up. He opened the door
and there was the postman
dressed as a rabbit.

Thinking it over while eating his bran flakes
he carried right on – as if
nothing had been – as if –

Even at work he was not quite himself
and Miss Grace, who was naked,
except for her shoes,

closely resembled an Orphic nymph.
Thinking it over, ensconced in his office,
he put down his glasses and looked at the ceiling

which opened into a neat black square
revealing the moon and Cassiopeia
and somebody fingering *Für Elise*.

Thinking it over during the morning
he made it to lunchtime –
wafer-thin ham with buttered ambrosia

and freshly-squeezed ice. He weighed all his options,
noted a comet
and reached a decision *not* to remark.

At quarter past five he placed all the pawpaws
into his briefcase
and travelled straight home on the Altrincham train

which was packed with commuters
and lions and cheetahs –
no seat to be had.

He was glad to get off
with a catch, with a sigh, with a sob of relief
and enter the hall of his own maisonette

to a tropical beach, its warm little waves
overwhelming the carpet.
He did not consider – not for a moment –

he stepped right inside
he stepped right inside
he stepped right inside

closed the front door
and took off his tie.

# The Answer

'What does it mean to you?' she asked
and I nearly bit my tongue, being about to say
*everything* and having to stop because how could that be right?
I thought about saying *it is my life*, but that was too extreme –
how can something be your life which may not be alive?
Besides, it's the people you love who matter most,
of course. People are more important than
anything else, because this is just words,
isn't it, and only words,
and ever and always
only words?

# Teller

Umbrella-ed here in Autumn light
I tell my story to the rain.

The rain goes tiptoe to the trees
and tells my life to leaves and moss.

The bark recounts, but not quite right,
the plot and counter-plot of loss.

I listen to the empty breeze
and start to tell my tale again.

# The Visitors

'Where are you going? Where are you from?
   Who is this man at your side?
He does not carry a wedding-ring
   and you are no bride.

'Speak. Speak. The rain beats down.
   Speak to me, friend or foe.
What do you look for at this hour?
   Where would you go?'

'I come from the past,' the woman says,
   'and I know not by what whim
I married a man who loved me more
   than I did him.

'It did not last. I fell in love
   with another then,' says she
'and he loved me well, but I loved him more
   than he did me.

'I left alone and travelled on
   with loss my only guide
until this drear companion
   fell in beside.

'Together we have missed the way.
   Together we would find
a hearth, a lamp, a loving heart
   and peace of mind.'

'Come in, come in,' says the clergyman
    'for you shall have my bed
and my own safe seat by the chimney fire
    and soup and bread.'

'She cannot come in,' her helpmeet sighs
    (his voice is like a ghost).
'She must regret what she can't forget
    and go unblest.'

'I cannot come in,' she says, and turns
    to the road with empty will
and hand in hand they breast the dark
    and loveless hill.

# Pattern

Every morning I wake.
Then I turn to the window and look
and when I can see the silver birch
I get up.

Later, in the evening, I turn back
to the bed, the pillow, the open book
and soon, because of sleep or the dark,
I get in.

Again and again. It's that simple.
I get up, I return, I get up, I return.
So it goes on.

In this room my bed expands:
here lies a man.
His life is slow as coral, swift as sand.
He puts it in my hands.

# Comforters

*For we are all around*
*and our bodies are made of light.*

Then what does the door mean?

The door is for entering the human frame,
entering and living.

And the window?

The window is for seeing partly,
and the way home.

And the glass of wine?

It attends to the beautiful and the lost,
it is the end of the world, and the beginning.

*For we are all around*
*and our bodies are made of light.*

# Putting Words in Your Mouth

Imagine you're my assistant, my trusted assistant
and we're going to make a poem –
the kind you repeat under your breath
on the train or driving or at night alone.
I'll give you the words, one by one.
Could you put them in your mouth and hold them there
please? Check the weight, width, taste and texture,
then speak them in strings like natural pearls
but not till I say.

                     I found the first eight
in a waste basket years ago:
*I think only, I think only of you*
Try them for size.
*I think only, I think only of you*
How do they feel? A little fervent perhaps,
leaning on the *only* as if someone is lonely.

*And the old words please me best*
That's your next string. Keep them together,
and add these few: *Lovers can't say anything new*

Which is true, is it not? So what have we got
in your mouth so far?
*I think only, I think only of you*
*And the old words please me best:*
*Lovers can't say anything new*

I love you for holding
the words in your mouth. Be good to the words,
to the seed pearls. The first line repeats:

*I think only, I think only of you –*

then

*True as a heart-beat, always true*
*To my sweetheart, to my absent guest*

*Sweet heart* – roll the words round. Brood over
the absent guest. Is he alive? Is he dead?
The words are for him but he isn't there.
*True as a heart-beat, always true*
*To my sweetheart, to my absent guest*

Is she mad? Does she care?
She retraces her steps:
*I think only, I think only of you*
*And the old words please me best.*

And now dear assistant, the whole set.
Say them like singing, plainsong, no antics.

*I think only, I think only of you*
*And the old words please me best.*
*Lovers can't say anything new:*
*I think only, I think only of you,*
*True as a heart-beat, always true*
*To my sweetheart, to my absent guest:*
*I think only, I think only of you,*
*And the old words please me best.*

# The Ballad of Ballantoul Burn

I would give my darling all I had,
    all that I had and more
if he would lift his heavy head,
    open the heavy door.

I would give my darling the box of songs
    and its little silver key
if he would raise his heavy eyes,
    and sing again for me.

I would bring him shoes to dance the reel
    and a shirt of cotton lawn,
a handsome kilt of good Scots wool –
    if he would put them on.

I gave my darling all I had,
    the best my gold could buy.
In sorrow he has drowned my good,
    in sorrow we must lie.

I gave my darling all I had.
    O how shall we make shift?
He has given me all his full heart's grief –
    it is a heavy gift.

# The Good Wife

I do not want to love this man
but I will love him if I can
or for a day or mortal span.

His lying in bed I do not love.
I cannot soilèd sheets approve
in phoenix or in turtle dove.

Only I care not to betray
the light on his skin at break of day,
the light on his skin at close of day

and so I love and loving stay.

# Gone

Our neighbour went to hospital –
'Back soon,' she said and so
we like to think she hasn't gone
where the dead men, dead men go.

She smiled and waved, her face was bright,
her illness didn't show.
But the blinds are drawn
and the light's not on.
It looks very much as though
she's gone where the dead men
    gone where the dead men
    gone where the dead men go.

We should have wished her well. Fare *well*.
It's quiet here, although
through the walls we hear
too clear, too clear
the phone unanswered. No
    we think she's gone,
    she must have gone
    where the dead men, dead men go.

Within her empty garden
a wind begins to blow
and the dust spins white
as the stones recite
the names of the dead we know
    and the dead men breed
    and the dead men seed
    and the dead men grow and grow.

# Garden of Love

I like gardening. Since I am God
I can decide – inside these fences –
who lives, who dies, whose will is denied.
Pansies worship me, faces
pleading for light, more light. Nature
permits some running to seed,
some carelessness in omnipotent care.
Let rain beat them down.

They rise again, encouraged by sun.
I rip to the bone, uproot the worst.
Bindweed, buttercups, coltsfoot – gone.
This thistle shall live. As I gripped it
my glove slipped. It hurt me the most
I can recall. I know I exist.

# The Kiss

Then we lay in silence. A kiss flew in
and circled the room. Ignoring our pain,
it skirted the lamp three times, swooped high,
tried to get out. *No,* said the window,
batting it low. We hardly dared breathe.
Oh but it lighted on your mouth
and you turned in uncertainty to me
and I took the kiss, took it willingly,
thinking of nothing to do with love
but relief at last. How could it leave
when we needed it? That whole day
the kiss stayed.

# Remembering the Way

I drive to town. I do it every day
through Cluny, past the road to Cardenden,
and by some miracle I know the way –
I know it daily. Filed inside my brain
the left-hand bend, the farm track on the right,
the row of cottages, the half-built barn,
the view across the fields, that sudden light
across the whole of Fife – the distances

                         the distances

till black as ice, what was familiar slips
to strange. Alien corn. Hawthorn. No sign,
no clue, no sane device. The foreign cars
are overtaking. Lost and displaced, alas

                         although

it doesn't last. I'm back. I know the way.
Today I know the way. Today I know.

# Gate Keeper

What can Age say to Youth
   about love, about truth,
that hasn't been sung
   when Age was still young?

With a smile and a sigh
   Age starts to reply
but lingers a while
   by the elderly stile.

To be properly heard
   he needs the right word.
Some time then, for thought.
   But a day is too short –

it takes half a year
   for the phrase to concur
and Youth – who can't wait –
   jumps the barred gate.

# Felis Infelix

All her possessions were left to me
who saw her off. There weren't many:
the basket in which she made her last journey,
a little bed, a litter tray (clean),
an old blanket, one toy lion,
some uneaten biscuits. Nothing of note.
She wore her futilely fine fur coat.

# Plainsong

the rain slipping soft from silent air
sings as it leaves the empty hills

blethers in ditch and lonely glen
dithers in brake and stony burn
slithers in spate and lazy foam
*well-wishing well-wishing well-wishing well*

*to the sea to the sea to the open sea*
which sings of the air, of the air to be

# The Size of Grief

Day one. Small. Stunned.
Day two, almost new.
A daze of days.

Then it's three hundred
and sixty five
and it's alive.

They speak of
'getting over it', they talk of
'getting through'

as if you could do
that. It is impassable

and simple as a leaf.
One side is black and it is grief.
The other (the green side) is love.

# Proof

When the small turboprop with me in it
lifts off the ground it is not a miracle,
only a miraculous fact.

And the tiny shadow
of the aeroplane on the clouds
flying inside a circular rainbow
isn't a miracle either,
just a marvellous phenomenon.

O when was the sky ever so blue?
The moon's face cracks with delight.

## Auchterawe Wood

This is how it is in word:
wind, water, wet, wood.

Filling, jurgling roll of stone,
bird needle, flute of bone:
this is how it is by ear.

Deep and dark. Viridian.
Flash of splash of falling light:
this is how it is by eye.

Cheek of ice, feather breath,
spat of wet, fluff of glove:
this is how it is by touch.

Sharp sap, mulch and pine,
art of wood-smoke, O of nowhere:
this is how by nose and tongue.

The wind, the wood, and hand in hand:
this is how it is by heart.

# Just This

Late in the evening sun
food is very good.
We are hungry, both of us:
we make short work of it.

The dining table shines.
Never a time more sweet
only to sit like this,
only to sit and eat.

## At Last

*Vaster than empires*, he thinks,
*and more slow*
as the huge tiredness comes
and minutes open like tombs.

*Later flowers for the bees*
he says, as time eases
and space *tick* yaws

but the dickory clock
has no tick –
it must be his heart.
*Dere hert*, he softly says,
*howe like you this?*

Slower than empires
and more vast,
the tiredness, the tiredness.

# A Picture of Forgetting

It's a dream, and you can't remember.
You search your mind for hope.
It's white as an envelope
but inside there's no letter.

You wake up. It's all right.
The painting of trees you love
is safe on your bedroom wall
illumined by the moon.

So sleep. Soon it's morning.
You remember not-remembering
though memory fades with light.
You glance again at the picture

not seeing the missing tree
which stole away in the night.
Soon other things will go.
You probably won't know.

The picture is called 'Forgetting'.
You will forget this too.
How beautiful is white.
You love the painting of snow.

# Landlubber's Song

*i.m. Stewart Eglin*

*O livery livery liver-me-lee*
*Give me a long, long liver.*

Merry O sherry, cheery with beer,
Timbers a shuddery shiver,
Toxins and poxins flushed out like dioxins
Thanks to my livery liver.

*O livery livery liver-me-lee*
*Give me a long, long liver.*

Perry O fine; port O divine:
Drink it from morning to quiver,
Never the sort to waste but a thought
On a privily snivelly liver.

*O livery livery liver-me-lee*
*Give me a long, long liver.*

Brandy and shandy and Armagnac!
Sing to the moon Moon River!
Soon the boon of the afternoon
Oblivionates an obliver.

*O livery livery liver-me-lee*
*Give me a long, long liver.*

Whisky lubberly, lubberly loo –
O for the now or niver –
Singing O liver, O liver my love,
Leave me or lose me foriver.

*O livery livery liver-me-lee*
*Give me a long, long liver.*

Up spak a daughter: 'Drink water,' says she.
'Take it with cake (O a sliver).
The past is away, the future's next week.'
Cheers to the answer I give her:

'Come along liver, O liver my love
Shape up O liver, old liver.'

*O livery livery liver-me-lee*
*Give me a long, long liver.*

# The Hill

His heart is okay (it has been checked)
but not far from the top his pace is checked

and he stops. 'Enough. Let's go back.'
She doesn't want to go back.

If they get to the summit, they'll see the view.
He doesn't give tuppence about the view.

'It's not far,' she says. 'Too far,' he says.
She doesn't care a bit what he says,

she wants to get to the top of the hill. 'Come on,'
she says, 'Best foot forward.'
                              'You go on,'

he replies. 'I'll wait here.' So she walks on her own
and quickly sets up a pace of her own

not hesitating and not looking back
until all at once she stops and looks back

and he's quite out of sight, could be anywhere
and a sort of fear catches her where

head and heart meet. This stupid emotion is love,
and because of that, because of her love,

if he won't get to the top of the hill,
then she won't get to the top of the hill

either. Anyway a few drops of rain
fall on her hair and she knows he hates rain.

He might even have turned
and gone home without her. She turns

and half-runs down the path. He is waiting for her,
sitting on his coat and waiting for her.

'About time', he says. 'Where have you been?'
She says, 'Where do you think I've been?

He doesn't ask about the view from the top.
She doesn't tell him she didn't get to the top.

She might think, 'This is the story of my life'
but although this is the story of her life

that is not what she thinks.
She thinks something else.

# Seer

He reached for me
and I saw and I saw
not his arm at all
but a smooth thin pole,
a spread flipper,
a furless claw –

and I saw and I saw
two trembling things
(someone said *legs*)
like saplings stripped
and flattening out
to a kind of a hinge
like a flange to the floor
where a (someone said) *foot*
was splayed at the root
in tubelets of flesh –

and O it was fact,
I saw now I saw
we were trapped inside bodies,
we could not get out.
Why did I have to
remember it?

# Blight

Each of us is old
and our brave silks begin
to fall from us. Draw close
in the chapterhouse of skin.

How shall we be glad?
We were young, young – we knew
it would happen as it happens
but not like this. Not to

us, not to the silk-sellers,
the bearers of spice and gold.
Our tales were bright in the telling
but this was not foretold.

# Duel

Your false self says to my true self, 'Hate'.
My true self says to your false self, 'No'.

Your false self says to my false self, 'Shit'.
My false self says to your false self, 'Go'.

Your true self says to my false self, 'Love'.
My false self says to your true self, 'Late'.

Late, too late, too late, too late.
My true self sings to your true self, 'Wait'.

# Fairy Tale

Out of the woods I walked with my axe.
The sky was impossibly blue.
A whisper of smoke from the chimney-stack
was a sign. But I already knew

this was the place. Lining the track
violets like certainty grew.
The end of all longing, the end of all lack:
the place I had found was you.

Through the window I glimpsed the flames,
a table laid ready for two.
I knocked on the door. You opened your arms.
It was true. It was really true.

Like coming home to reality
after a life-time away,
if the woman beside you had just been me.
She wasn't. I didn't stay.

Like mortal pain. Like confusion
of form and fact. Like I said
(now we've dispensed with illusion)
the Babes in the Wood are dead.

# Preoccupation

Swallow it. Down the throat, slick
quick – gone. Call it Sin.

It will sleep for years, somewhere
between angel and kidney. Then stir.

Seething and impure, blood-hot
is the mind's meat. It can wait.

## Secret

Summer rain at midnight
sweetens the wakeful air.
You won't forget, you can't forget
nowhere is everywhere.

Still the rain is singing:
love watches over despair.
I've put this into words for you
so you can keep it there.

# Epistle to Angus Calder

And as for living inside this verse,
you know that is utter shite.
Poems can't hold a human hand
or put an absence right.
Life is what skulks in a city flat,
drawing the blinds at night.

At least your name remains the same,
worthy protagonist still
to gods and sods and demons.
Hang on, old friend until
you can remember, bit by bit,
everything. Drink your fill

of all that is and all that was
and all that's about to begin.
The Test Match awaits your verdict:
someone is going to win,
and later the best of words will call
and Calder will be in.

# The Book of the Night

has black pages.
Its words are horses
light years away.
Grey woman
get on and ride.

*Are there stories?* Oh yes,
but you may not like them.
Too many floors,
too many stairs.

*And stars?* Indeed,
but you cannot see them.
Grey woman
put out the light.

*Angels?*
Perhaps. Soon
you'll find out.

Come on. It's time.
Put on your gown.
Grey woman
come away down.

*Put out the light?*
Put out the light.
They all fall.
It is all right.

# Making the Bed

Untroubled by unachieved desire
I make the rumpled bed. I like
the sheets' precision, so I take
my efforts as a metaphor

for equanimity sustained
by work in hand. Enduring yet
in sober fold and careful pleat
and stroke and tuck and counterpane,

the thing untold is safely sleeved,
its creases smoothed and patted down.
Untroubled by desire achieved
the pillows sigh. The quilt sleeps on.